knee deep in high water

01 02 03 04 05 27 26 25 24 23

Caitlin Press Inc.
3375 Ponderosa Way
Qualicum Beach, BC V9K 2J8
www.caitlinpress.com

Text and cover design by Sarah Corsie
Cover artwork by Deryk Houston
Printed in Canada

Caitlin Press Inc. acknowledges financial support from the Government of Canada and the Canada Council for the Arts, and the Province of British Columbia through the British Columbia Arts Council and the Book Publisher's Tax Credit.

Library and Archives Canada Cataloguing in Publication

Knee deep in high water : riding the Muskwa-Kechika, expedition poems / Bronwyn Preece.
Names: Preece, Bronwyn, 1978– author.
Identifiers: Canadiana 20230156568 | ISBN 9781773861142 (softcover)
Classification: LCC PS8631.R425 K54 2023 | DDC C811/.6—dc23

knee deep in high water :

    riding the Muskwa-Kechika

expedition poems

bronwyn preece

Caitlin Press 2023

for Christy Drever,
physiotherapist extraordinaire ...
all i can say is thank you. thank you. and thank you! none of this would
have been possible without you ...

for Janis McLean,
for the utterly rich and endlessly rewarding friendship ... and the occasional surprise gift of a beloved book in the mail!

for Wayne Sawchuk,
for making me appreciate the notion of 'giddy-up!' in so many more
ways than one ... beyond grateful!

of note :

these poems reflect one woman's personal experience on an expedition with Muskwa-Kechika Adventures. the collection does not attempt to reflect others' experiences on the same trip in any way. the author holds the guide, fellow riders, wranglers/farriers and company as a whole with the utmost respect and in the highest esteem. i am forever grateful for the experience ...

•

i write in lowercase —
>out of respect, i capitalize all Indigenous references, the name of the expedition leader and the horses' names. i keep capitals in most citations from books and references.

i have done my utmost to fact check all of my references through various sources; however, i remain a visitor to the area i write about here within and i humbly apologize if i have gotten anything wrong ...

i would like to thank Vici Johnstone and Sarah Corsie of Caitlin Press for your support, thoroughness and thoughtfulness ... it has been nothing short of a pleasure working with you.

U

this is a collection of poems. a narrative. a journey, an experience, a story. penned in, and amongst, a mixture of saddles, stirrups, tents and tarps, melting mountains and rising rivers, thwarted plans, awe, overwhelm, and breathtake in the backcountry. it travels through many territories and ethical terrains. it is one woman's account of moving into deeper understandings of self, Peoples and place, as a person of predominantly settler-descent visiting unceded Ancestral Lands in northern british columbia. it is a documentation of these unfurling relationships, overlaps, challenges, hopes and their inextricable reveals *in situ*. the collection captures snippets, soundbites, moments, geology, geography, ornithological-envy, history and gaps.

this is my chronicling of a remote, two-week horse expedition, embarked upon while recovering from a leg-shattering injury, that left me with an acutely crooked knee.

in many ways it is a love story. it houses struggles and celebration. it becomes, and bears, witness ...

it is a book of longing and learning ...

of experiencing

and a return to the trail ...

1.

Kledo boat launch,
june 28, 2021

i am
Muskwa
Rivered,
        loading
into jetboat,

array of
        orange, black, green
dry bags ...

i am
an hour
past mile 300
of the alaskan
highway –
a place which
competes for
the title of *'oldest*
white settlement
in bc',[1]

where the land
speaks in
shadows,

song of *Dene,*
Nêhiyawêwin,
Kaska Dena ...
rooting itself in
Slavey/Cree
tones, terms,
Territory :

my desire to accord proper Territorial acknowledgment to this area
— where i find myself privileged to be a visitor — is met with a painful his-
tory of forced removal, division of bands, conquering containment and
re-patriation ...

it becomes hard to detangle the destructive colonial legacy from the
rightful associations : Traditional Territories overlapped, being seasonally
nomadic Peoples. the imposition of reserves defiled lineages of symbi-
otic subsistence, survival and spiritual sustenance ... and yet, despite
governmental-instituted regimes of attempted genocide, many of the
surviving Peoples forming part of Treaty 8, including the Fort Nelson
First Nation, call these lands 'home' ...

*'The Crown recognized the territorial and jurisdictional rights of our people
within the boundaries of Treaty No. 8, as demonstrated by the Crown enter-
ing into treaty with the Fort Nelson Slavey on August 15, 1910, in the form
of an adhesion to Treaty No. 8, signed on the banks of the Fort Nelson River
at Old Fort Nelson. [...]*

*We have rights and privileges under the provisions of said Treaty including,
amongst others, access to and benefit of the resources within our traditional
territory of said Treaty "for as long as the sun shines, the grass grows and
the rivers flow".*[2]

this river, Muskwa, means black bear.[3]

i have been
early-morning
shuttled here,
from fort nelson
to water's edge,

by the boat operator,
in a 4x4 super-duty.

we talk
pipelines, hunting,

burning, wolves,
caribou. *and*
clouds.

we speak
northern.

i board the boat.

> *only days before,*

> > i purposely poured
> > my coffee into my
> > expedition-embossed
> > mug. downed it, drowned
> > the plants, unplugged
> > the kettle, chucked
> > the garbage, locked
> > the door, hid the
> > key. *and set the*
> > *odometer to 0.*

> > backseat overflowing.
> > full tank of gas.
> > fresh oil change.
> > *and* four new tires.

> > first stop,
> > a friend's. i sound-
> > track the appropriate
> > song for the three
> > kilometre drive :

> > > with lyrics that suggest
> > > i may be able to
> > > lessen the depressive load
> > > of another by just showing up.
> > > *a weight-lifter.*

i fix us
coffee.
i have been
coming here
every day for
two weeks.
showing up.
now i am
leaving
for three ...

backing out
the door,
i clench my fist
to my chest,
'you got this'

though
directed at him,
i'm speaking to
the both
of us ...

i put on
my shades,
picking them up
off my dashboard
littered with
mementos from
past road trips :
        sand dollar, antler,
           incense ... and
a left-under-the-
windshield-found-
note : *'you are*
beautiful'

i reverse

out of the
driveway
and deliberately
remove the
song – 'burden'[4] – from
my playlist.

i try to
shift gears

> *(my car is an*
> *automatic).*

it's an overcast
heatwave

> *i'm already*
> *present to the*
> *metaphors and*

i haven't even
left yet.

i am
about to
ascend eight
parallels :
> a latitudinal
> journey in
> longitude

riding shotgun :
books.
> *muskwa-kechika : the wild*
> *heart of canada's northern rockies,*[5]
>> the akrigg's *british*
>> *columbia place names*[6]
> and *geology of british columbia : a journey*
> *through time*[7]

plus *summer*
of the horse[8]

    twinning
    cordilleran
    backbones
    with the inter-
    montane, i
    become
    traveller of
    plateau, plains
    and prairie

i cue
up 'the ultimate
outdoorswoman'[9]

    peaks yield
    to haybales
    and homesteads,
    red gambrels and
    foothills,

i subsist
on a diet of
avocados and
drive-thru cups,

washing socks
and sundress
in hotel sinks :
    williams lake
    dawson creek
    and fort nowhere
        [as an ex-boyfriend
        texted back with a shocked
        question mark,
        upon my dropping
        him a pin]

i drive
through semi-
skid, rubber
blow-out ...

    and the
    single red
    dress hanging
    from a roadside
    tree

wildlife corridors

    i had
    no spare change
    for the woman
    asking of me ...

'for the next
454 km continue
straight'

industry
flares its
signposts

    'crews and
    hunters welcome'

bug splat
coats grill,
windshield :

    i become
    undulation
    of crook
    and turn

a solo

right-of-passage

in this
vastness,

on this
strip of
road

.

.

.

i pull into
my small
(non)destination
town. i have
tipped 1,500 km.

[i buy a camo hat]

at river's
edge,
saddles,
coolers, coca-
cola, country
music and a
handful of stetson-
wearers
board the jetboat, too.

we will
be travelling for
four hours, forty
miles up the
Muskwa, forty
miles up the
Tuchodi, to the

lake of the same name :

'the place of
big water'[10]

meeting up
with twenty-one
horses and two
wrangling-farriers.
we will replace
the outgoing riders.

a packstring
expedition :

we will ford river,
commence a multi-day mountain pass
ascent and traverse, explore valleys,
ride the High Trail and reach the Gathto

over the next
fifteen days,
i will get
to know
my fellow
riders :
-*the retired marine biologist, seaweed specialist, strategic planner, tran-*
scendental meditator, on the cusp of his 75th birthday and on his
nineteenth trip with the packtrain;
-*the retired arctic-going hydrographic launch jockey, former model and music*
therapist, on her third expedition, about to turn 70 and currently a
long-distance, high-speed motorcyclist, well-versed in the I Ching;
-*the retired medical tech, environmental and nutritional consultant: 'all sci-*
ence', gulf islands gardener, who brought with her the book 'plants of
northern british columbia'. she also happens to be knower of many
bird calls and songs, on her fifth trip at the age of 70;
-*the weather-station monitoring highways-worker, skier, canoe poler and*

tracker, former whitewater kayaker, helicopter crash survivor, moose-
meat provider, on his third trip into these mountains, and about to
reach the milestone of 50;
-the two all-around horse-whispering, wrangling, shoeing and camp coor-
dinating experts, infinitely patient and helpful, both in their late
twenties,

each having worked with these horses, respectively, for more than
nine years :

one female : articulate, bad-ass in the most intelligent, compassion-
ate and supportive ways, tattooed, social justice advocate, proudly
Métis and expert Bannock maker

one male : bearded and bespectacled, calm, resourceful, great
tall-tale-teller, search-and-rescue member, an avid reader of history,
knower of many random facts and for who i am grateful for having
been a necessary walking-stick-whittler

-and Wayne Sawchuk :
guide, outfitter, hunter, tender of trapline, visionary conservation-
ist, writer ...

and the reason i came, and have come, to be here.

we motor
through
pushback of
silty-brown to pewter
to glacial blue,

banks scoured
by time's layers

shaled, streaked,
scratched, scored
and scarred

navigating
upstream :

    the present
    moment
    feels like
    driving in reverse,
    moving forward

        [harnessed by
        sitting a 425-
        horsepower ride]

exposing,

    being exposed

to history's
coursing,

    eroding
filaments

    etched
thrust and
folded

the sky burns

river beauty
blooms

then ...
    the lake

and camp

on the 'spine of the continent' :

a single loon calls

and this woman,
                solo
begins to bleed ...

2.

i am
jagged

outline of
cloudless
morning

boundaries blurring
definitions of the
finite, precipice,
edge,
        of the
ethereal …

lighting a
continuum drawn
between dusk
and dawn

contours glow

colours,
        the possession
        of pigmented patents

my tent
rests feet from the
bank of a shore-since-
recently-and-
rapidly-disappeared

nooked
by white spruce
amongst bloom
of rose,

marked by manure
and silver berry-
wolf willow

and cross-lake push, wrap
and ply of peaks ...

trembling aspens
fondle canopy

as
chop of
firewood splits
the calm with
a few kindling
swings. *break-*

fast sounds.

i have
barely caught up
on road-trip stolen
sleep,
thieved by
near twenty-
four-hour days.
sunrise and
sunset inter-
lacing their
soon-to-be-solstice
embrace through
tether of a mere
few hours of
twilight. *headlamps*
not required.

yesterday's
already-high water
has risen even
higher. the
surge in record-
breaking heat :

    transforming
    glaciers

into torrents of
run-off,

    delaying
    our plans.

the river cannot
be forded at
these levels,
even with
horses. we
are '*essentially*
marooned,' Wayne
remarks.

    expedition at full halt
    (and we haven't even mounted yet)

i wade
in
and collect water

    '*The Muskwa-Kechika Management Area (M-KMA), situated in northern*
    British Columbia, Canada, is a globally significant area of wilderness, wildlife
    and cultures, to be maintained in perpetuity, where world class integrated
    resource management decision-making is practiced ensuring that resource
    development and other human activities take place in harmony with

wilderness quality, wildlife and dynamic ecosystems on which they depend. The M-KMA was designated in legislation (M-KMA Act, 1998). [...] The M-KMA includes Parks and Protected Areas where resource extraction is prohibited, and management zones where resource extraction may occur, according to higher standards than elsewhere in the province. [...] Few places on earth match the significance of the Muskwa-Kechika Management Area (M-KMA) in terms of raw beauty, isolation, biodiversity, wildlife, wilderness, natural resources and spiritual and cultural value. The Muskwa-Kechika (musk-quah-ke-chee-kah) Management Area is an innovative management system, named for two major rivers that flow through the area, that was developed through a public planning process. [...] Translated, Muskwa means Bear and Kechika (Ketchika - Táhdáséh) means long inclining river. [...] The M-KMA lies in the traditional territories of the Kaska Dena, Treaty 8 and Carrier-Sekani. The following are First Nations Communities found within or adjacent to the M-KMA :

Treaty 8 First Nations

- *Halfway River First Nation*
- *Prophet River First Nation*
- *Fort Nelson First Nation*

Kaska Dena First Nations

- *Kwadacha First Nation*
- *Daylu Dena Council*
- *Dease River First Nation*
- *Fireside*
- *Muncho Lake*

Carrier-Sekani

- *Tsay Keh (say-kay) Dene*

The Muskwa-Kechika comprises an area of 6.4 million hectares'.[11]

.
.
.

the iron
skillet sears
eggs, bacon and
leftover potatoes
from last night's supper
of rib-eyes and wine,
over the central fire.
i partook
in the first-night
communality of
melmac-served-
merlot, steak and
veg. here on in,
however, i will
be taking care
of my own food.
          [my diet : not carb-
          heavy, camp-food friendly]

i remove
blackened kettle
from grill with
a stick. i measure
out my mixture
of coffee, collagen,
and coconut creamer.

camp life
pivots around
the ground-level
fire *(until soon-to-be-learned-of*
fire restrictions
curb this practice).
an assembly of folding chairs, a
collapsible table covered in duct-
taped-sealed condiments and
plastic plates surround.
tubs for washing
dishes in sequence and

campsuds
frame the sides.
a line of panniers[12]
rim another, with a
canvas-covered mound of rope-
wrapped tack parcels and blankets
squaring off the
edge.

upon arrival,
yesterday, the
horses were all
nearby. seeking shade.
bells around several
of their necks.
this morning,
they have hobbled[13]
off. they are later
located about five
or six kilometres away.

we will
ride tomorrow :

      a day trip
      on *this* side of the
      shoreless lake, *this* side of
      the river's rapid rising.

i settle
into the
morning
conversation of
bird calls and
politics, slaughter
house poundage
pricing and stories

of the local turn-of-
the-century *bedaux*
and *henry* missions.

the swainson's
thrush is identified.
call and song. Wayne
points out a tree shredded by
grizzly claw.

i set off on a walk
with two-cum-
three others. we
pass wolf scat,
spot cinquefoil,
creamy peavine,
round-leaved orchid,
twinflower, twin-
berry, twisted
stalk and mountain
death-camas. northern
goldenrod, grass-of-
parnassus and
geranium. just
as pioneer mary henry
did ...
            Wayne tells of how botanical
            samples she collected
            on the edge of Tuchodi Lake
            in the early 1930s
            are still propagated at,
            and by,
            the henry foundation,[14]
            in the eastern states.

            i make note of
            wanting to visit.[15]

flooding
overtakes
the trail

pine siskin alerts the air.

i ask
about the
practice of
burning the
garbage. *even*
the plastic. i had
anticipated cacheing it
and packing it out.
'to protect the bears,' Wayne
straightforwardly replies.

my wrapper goes
up in flames.

i first met Wayne Sawchuk in 2017 at a five-day hybrid writing residency titled *enlichenment, enlivenment and the poetics of place* in *wells gray, british columbia.* the residency brought together professional writers, artists and scientists from across the country to engage in timely, exploratory, creative collaboration. Sawchuk was instrumental in garnering protected-status for the precariously fragile and environmentally-threatened Muskwa-Kechika [MK] in the 1990's. his visionary advocacy earned him a national environmental award. currently, the pressures of hydroelectric and mining interests are proving formidable, challenging the strength and loopholes held within the designation of 'protected.' 'Sawchuk has been leading expeditions into the remotest regions of the MK for decades as part of an effort to protect this magnificent area.'[16] meeting Wayne – in the context of that residency – instilled a deep desire to one-day have the opportunity to join him on a packhorse expedition, as both a *writer* and *witness.*

and now

here

i was,

    i am,

with
Wayne Sawchuk as my guide ...

Wayne has been
visiting this
roughed-out camp
for more than
thirty years. he
understands
this place. *he
belongs here.*

i pour over
my *pocket
naturalist* plants
pamphlet and the
pojar & mackinnon
volume.
i had read-up about
mary henry before
coming ... *sepia-
tinged paper-turned-
pdf from archival
tomes ...*

Mary Gibson Henry was an American, city-bred, pioneering amateur botanist
and horticulturalist, born in 1884. She spent four summers over the period
of 1931-1934 exploring the northern rocky mountains with multi-month
packtrain expeditions. 'Very little was known about the Northern Rockies of
Canada before World War II and before the construction of the Alaska High-

way. Early fur traders had followed the two great rivers, the Liard and the Peace, through the Rockies and had established small centres dependent on trapping. [...] In the 1930s, the lands between the two great rivers became a challenge to the venturesome. Addressing this challenge came an unlikely adventurer [...] In 1931, Mary Henry [...] heard from a trapper that there was a "tropical" valley to the north. It was curiosity about the plants which might grow there which led her to the expedition of 1931. [...T]ravel in the north it was stated, would be fraught with formidable obstacles and should not be attempted. Nevertheless she was determined to go ..."[17]

here, i now was : botanical books in hand.

Wayne spoke
with mary henry's grandson.
he had few good
things to say
about the matriarch,
reporting she
was a battle-
axe. *she was
one fierce woman.*

    'you'd have to be,
    out here,'
        i unequivocally
        remark.

Wayne would
later guide mary's
granddaughter around
the Tuchodis ... as she
wished to retrace
trekked lines of
[her]
lineage ...

i consider

the curve of time

the land around me blooms.

i go
for a swim
amongst winded,
white-capping,
surrounded by
'unnamed' peaks ...

Indigenous legacy
draws this place
into the now :

immerses this
hold,
this ground :

fire stones, adzed
tools.

artefacts
not the possession
of a past,
but the embedment
of presence,
a vital
acknowledgement
of the animacy
of Aboriginality ...

(re)tracing
pathways

and yet,
colonialism's
influence reigns :
    Peoples dis-placed,
    migratory populations
    dwindling, animal
    routing changing …
    lakes and rivers
    rising, while
    the exploitative
    lens of industry
    hones its scope :
        predatorily targeting
        expansion for
        resource extraction.

landscape,
thus, *becomes*
(further)
precarious,
vulnerable

    affected

could my experiencing
be considered
an 'encounter with
an absence'?[18]

'the human
race is a
constant
disappointment,'

Wayne quips
from across
the fire,
in response
to something
else,
        but its
timely applicability
couldn't be more
appropriate.

i look
up, *however,*
and find
a group of
people i
already consider
friends. *like-
minded folks.*

the evening
gathers
cumulous,

and

two of
us go
launch
a canoe …

3.

i am
awake to
feel the first
drop of rain
through mesh

> *a 4:30 a.m.*
> *affix-of-fly*
> *to tent,*

by five, the
pelting is a
steady score of
atmospheric
release. *relief.*
the weather has
broken. by six-
thirty, all has,
once again,
dispersed —

> re-absorbed into
> glint of spotless
> reflection. *mirrored*
> *stillness.* it's
> seamlessly clear.
> sun illuminating
> suspension of
> gibbous quarter
> moon.

a fish leaps.

'here come the steeds.'

bells of beating
hooves approach.

i've got on my (man's)
flannel, pearly buttons
and push-up bra.

i meet Antoinette,
Toni.
my horse :

        dappled, bay
        roan, with a
        dark dorsal stripe
        running the length of
        her back. raised
        from a foal by Wayne,
        some twenty-five years
        ago, *or so* ...
                these
        trails are syncopated
        with the trajectories
        of her chambered
        heart,
            her being ...

this,
her backyard.

she has
gentle eyes

a floral concho
bejewels her
bridle, reminiscent
of chipped-
enamel-decades-
old-farmhouse-
kitchenware :

matron mare

she wears
a bit-less
hackamore

she holds
strong opinions.

pad, then blanket placed.
saddle cinched, stirrups
raised (my 5'4¾" requiring extra
perforations), saddle bags
filled. lead rope half-
hitched twice around
the horn.

leather gloves on.

i am
able to
successfully
mount on
the left. *even*
with *my* leg.

i put
on my
custom-made,
embroidered

backcountry
cowgirl

hat ...

      leading up to this moment,
      the joke has been :

            if i can't straighten my post-injury,
                  significantly angled-in crooked leg,
            if doctors can't, nor physio,
            then two weeks on a horse,
            may just damn well do it!

bowing western,

            awaiting a third, and hopefully,
            final surgery : a full knee replacement

i wrap around
Toni's roundness.

i follow
Wayne on
Bonus. we
are venturing
westward along
the upperside
of the lake.

we are
the first
through
this year.

Wayne necessarily
carries an axe.
he dismounts
frequently.

the single-
noted whistle
of varied thrush
and huffed surprise of
grouse
announce our passing

the packhorses
have stayed at camp.

honeysuckled,

the trail is flanked
by elk antler-
scathed bark and
cambium-seeking
bear,
track of ungulate,
droppings of stone sheep and
corralled remnants of
hunting camp ...

all
territorizing
our path

as does
an Indigenous
hearthstone ...

earlier this morning,
just Wayne and i,
sitting around
the simmer of coals,
savouring the last sips
of our grounds,

> i recount how
> i remember him relaying to the
> group in wells gray,
> the reason why we should not
> ring our fires
> with rocks. i ask him to
> tell me again.
> they demark
> an area – stake a claim –
> create a border
> synonymous
> with colonialist
> practices – that
> will leave an
> indelible impression on
> the landscape that
> will be discoverable
> in geologic records for
> millennia to come.

> *'and that's not*
> *the kind of mark*
> *you want to leave.'*

> they do nothing
> to contain the flames.

he tells me, Aboriginal Peoples
did not ring their
fires.

ours is
rimmed with
logs. it will
vanish.

the stone
we pass
radiates,
it doesn't ring.

.

this land
        is traplined.
        i ask of
        the breakdown
        between
        settler and
        Indigenous
        operations.
        Wayne calls back :
        'about fifty/fifty.'

we pass
old wooden
conibear trap
for wolverine.

suddenly,
one of our riders
and
horses tumble
sideways into
lake, as a high-
watered bank

gives way ...

    never before
    has Wayne seen
    the level so high.

THIS is what
change looks like,
        feels like

we become
watermarked
and marks ...

    feet eject
    from stirrups
    as all are forced
    to wade
    belly-deep

surrounded by

stripped
peaks –
    save a few
    couloirs of
    crevassed
    white –

sedimentary
skyscrapers

of sawn teeth
jutting upwards,

bare rock,

baring
      our modern times :

immemorially
rivuletted
and
rivuletting ...

slicing deep
into [the]
overhead

      verticalizing
      a horizon

      stripped naked.

the sky
begins to gather its
innocuous shades into an
etiolated weave of
opaque

we cross
alluvial
fan pushing
up *dryas,*
shrubbrush and
mountain avens. the
shrilled flight of
a single yellow-
legs dashes
above the waxen
coat of leaves.

we arrive,
some seven, eight,
nine kilometres
later at an
old outfitting cabin,
built post-WWII
by a group of american
army men.
        they aptly named it
        lac-a-nookie.

we stop
for lunch,

        exploring
        cast iron cookstove
        and wooden bunks.

Comet
Cassiar
Levi
Vern
Big Rig
Bonus and
Toni
        wait patiently.

eagle and
raven circle

coolness creeps
in, just in time
to be swamped
by the clam of
humidity,
        as

we turn
for home

i think
of my grandfathers.
one an english
fox-hunter and
caretaker of a royal
manor stable. one
a famed writer of
horse-mounted
westerns, *criminals*
and cowboys ...

    a warbler
    chortles the trees

and,
i settle
into my seat.

i explore
stretching possibilities,
whilst remaining
in full control on
the uneven. *flex*
up. flex down.
stand up, extend.
the slight bend
demanded of
both knees,
foreshortens
the gastrocnemius.
shins on fire.
core engaged,
posture erect,

i long
for the trots. *my*
leg hurts.

the packhorses
whinny our return.
    we have been
    gone some six+
    hours.

tack off,

      the pressing
      focus becomes
      erecting a tarp.

south-westerly
winds whip up
to gale-like force.
my tent, *though*
weighted with
gear, has been
pushed way back,
snagged in bush. i
fight to re-stake
the rippling nylon.

.

two stray
horses have
appeared, one
a colt. *both*
unshod. the

theory is they
became separated
from their downriver
free-roaming herd by
the rising waters
        inconclusive ideas
        are tossed around
        as to what to do ...

dry. we eat,
undercover.

and,
i send a
satellite message
to my daughter :

        lightning and
        booming thunder,
        horse bells and
        tea under a tarp
        next to the fire!

4.

i am
shadow sleeper

bedding
on an
eroded
mattress of
single-celled
skeletons,

   diatoms

planktonic, silica-
walled alga
fossilized in the
rising compression
of the Muskwa
Assemblage, *layered*
formations, the Chischa
housing the
oldest rocks
in the rockies.
   organic origins,
tectonostratigraphically-
speaking :

> 'Strata within the Mesoproterozoic Muskwa Assemblage in the Tuchodi
> Lakes area of northern British Columbia appear to have been developed by
> repeated progradation of storm-influenced carbonate and siliciclastic ramp
> facies over deeper water muds in an inner to outer shelf setting within an ex-
> tensional or transtensional basin. [...] The lowermost exposed strata in the
> Muskwa Assemblage are the Chischa Formation. This consists predominantly
> of fine grained dolomicrites, with stromatolites, flat-pebble conglomerates,
> gutter-casts and hummocky cross-stratification, indicating a shallow-water,
> storm-influenced ramp environment. Molar-tooth structures are abundant :
> these early pre-diagenetic features of enigmatic origin ...'[19]

here,
years measure
time in billions

    periods, eras,
    epochs, eons

my 15,853 days
on earth
still somehow
feel as if
they belong,
    i belong
despite my
in situ foreignness ...

here,
in the Muskwa-
Kechika, we are
in the *northern*
rocky mountains
provincial park :

    'established in June 1999, the park encompasses 665,709 hectares. it is the
    largest of all the parks in the Muskwa-Kechika and the third largest provin-
    cial park in british columbia.'[20]

today
is a forecast-
dictated
relax-round-the-fire,
multi-kettle morning,

followed by
an afternoon
reconnaissance
hike of the *past-and*
maybe-still-hopeful-

river-crossing site :

the expedition must go on!

we pass
hedysarum, pink
pyrola, aster,
bedstraw and
aged reminders of
former beaver activity.
past root-dig of ursus
arctos horribilis. we
move into lodgepole
pine, juniper. *we are*
kinnikinnicked and
soopolallied.
i am fortunate
to be with those
who get down
on their hands and
knees to smell
scent of ground-
cover. *those*
who scratch
beneath the surface ...

we stop
at an
ancient
encampment

we will
later find out
that canada
day has been
cancelled ...

the importance,
significance, and
profoundly poignant
move has *finally*
come ...

154 years too late.

i am
feelings
beyond
my vocabulary

.

.

.

beyond my age

.

.

.

beyond Time Immemorial

.

.

.

.

.

.

the river crossing
is, and will be,
impossible.

[*don't change horses midstream]

plans must change

we will
not reach the
Gathto, nor head
into the valley
Wayne has
yet ever to explore.

       we will,
       however −
              moored on this
              side of the lake,
              river and mountains −
       still
       be able to travel
       portions of the
       High Trail (the
       summer-winter
       route of the Dene
       and Kaska and
       suspected way,
              if indeed north
              america was
              populated by
              those travelling
              south down
              the ice-free corridor
              of the eastern
              rockies,
       that was taken)

the five

of us,
on river-
reconnaissance,
instead, head up.
hiking.
we will try to find
another trail system
to explore with the
horses, up the
rear ridge

      a detour —

a way to avoid
the washout
from dissolved
bank —
to move
downstream
to then
connect with
a trail up towards
the Chischa.

Wayne blazes
as we go.
we follow
game trails,
ranging in faintness and
distinction.
scat and bones
lead our
way. a bull moose,
blanched and
desiccated by
the bitterness
of winter, lies
next to radiant glow of

limestone-clinging lichen.
xanthoria elegans.
and, a single
red strawberry.

chipping sparrow calls

faint rain
begins.
an electric
flash is soon
chased by a roar.

we turn and
return
to camp,
some seven
kilometres later,
just in time
for light precipitation
to turn to
unleash of
torrential sheets.
      we huddle beneath
      tarp, edges sagging
      with cascades.
sitting close,
we can barely
hear one another.
      'this is flash
      flood weather.'
pails collect water. *yet,*
birdsong
can still be discerned.
odes to the
nearing pleasure

of worms.

in pink hunting-
motif gumboots
and impermeable
rubber raincoat,

i go check on my
tent. and my
hanging laundry,
on an extended
rinse cycle.

we dine. we play
botanical trivia.
we celebrate *un-*
canada day

          and

i ask more
about the People
of this Territory ...

> '*The true spirit and intent of [Treaty No. 8] was based upon principles of law, respect, honesty and acceptance, as told by our Elders past.*
>
> *Hailed as a Treaty of peace, co-existence and sharing, its signing was witnessed by the Creator through the smoking of the pipe. The Treaty has a comprehensive framework that allows First Nations and the newcomers to collectively uphold all the rights and privileges of Treaty No. 8. The Treaty promotes co-existence between peoples on the landbase and the sharing of the resources, both renewable and non-renewable.*'[21]

Declaration of BC Treaty 8 First Nations

Doig River First Nation, Fort Nelson First Nation, Halfway River First Nation, Prophet River First Nation, Saulteau First Nation, and West Moberly First Nations

The leadership of the BC Treaty 8 First Nations acknowledge this Accord as a landmark agreement that outlines the commitment to work together to protect, preserve and prosper on behalf of Treaty 8 First Nations and their membership.

WE, the Chiefs of the BC Treaty 8 First Nations, shall continue to honour and implement the true spirit and intent of Treaty No. 8 signed by our forefathers in 1899.

WE, the Chiefs of the BC Treaty 8 First Nations, continue to recognize that we have the inherent right to maintain the land and its resources through self governance which is based on our own sacred laws.

WE, the Chiefs of the BC Treaty 8 First Nations, affirm that our lands and resources were not surrendered or ceded to the Government of Canada.

WE, the Chiefs of the BC Treaty 8 First Nations, shall no longer allow the infringement of our Aboriginal and Treaty Rights. We recognize the need for and shall develop treaty conservation practices to manage, protect and defend our mode of life.

WE, the Chiefs of the BC Treaty 8 First Nations, will no longer allow resources to be extracted from our lands without meaningful consultation, revenue sharing or co-management practices. We will work together to create 'economic certainty' for all our communities, members and families.

WE, the Chiefs of the BC Treaty 8 First Nations, resolve to address the onslaught of development within Treaty 8 BC Lands by enhancing the Community Based Land Use Offices and developing a collective Land Use Support Office that will assist in the implementation regarding all aspects of T8 co-management opportunities.

WE, the Chiefs of the BC Treaty 8 First Nations, are determined to participate at the highest level of government, with both Canada and the Province, to create legislative changes that will promote true co-management that will enhance our way of life.

We, the Chiefs of BC Treaty 8 First Nations, shall exercise our inherent right to self-governance by becoming politically involved at the community, regional, provincial and national levels. We will strive to develop working relationships with all levels of Government and all stakeholders so that our voices can be heard and recognized.

WE, the Chiefs of the BC Treaty 8 First Nations, shall focus on developing solutions that will address cumulative impacts by designing a traditional model that will enhance land use planning and monitoring, supported by a T8 compliance and enforcement program.

WE, the Chiefs of the BC Treaty 8 First Nations, will commit to developing, preserving and promoting traditional and modern methods of education, which includes language, culture and traditional practices for our children, youth and Chiefs.

WE, the Chiefs of the BC Treaty 8 First Nations, will commit to setting aside all our cultural and personal conflicts and differences to stand united for the greater cause of securing a brighter future for all generations to come.

We, the Chiefs of BC Treaty 8 First Nations, acknowledge the original Accord that was drafted and agreed to in September 2003 is now being re-affirmed once again on June 21, 2006, the anniversary of our historical Treaty.[22]

5.

i am
hand-cup
of lake,

cleanse

set within
see-through
segments of
blue,

      potentiality

'are we ready?!
this, is exploring ...
this is what this is!'

chainsaw, two
axes and flagging
tape,

we are setting off
to cut trail.

no rifle.

we whistle
relay signals ...

      come this way
         (two blasts)

i'm coming back
        (single blast)

we fan out, we
follow, we group,
scout, *wayfind* ...

we swat.
mosquitoes pierce
my leggings, my
sleeves. they land
in droves, *proboscis
at-the-ready.* for
ease of movement,
i left my armour
of full rain gear in
my pack. *mistake.*
plus, the bushes
are still wet.

i am soaked.

we agree
to trail-find
first, clear
en route back.

we intersect a
variety of criss-crossing paths ...

        *some animal,
        some once-upon-
        humaned,* some
        free-ranged,

landing, in part,
on what was
likely an old fur

trapper's alternative
route.

i become
effusion of citronella and
essential oil.
insect in fold
of eye, in gap of teeth,
gaunt of cheek, behind
epiglottal flap,
canal of ear, knuckled
fold of knee, web
of thumb, under tongue,
caught within taut
tie of drawstring, and
crack of ... *yes,* even
there.

lousewort, lupine,
high-bush cranberry
and wetland equisetum.
cotton grass, pussytoes
and gooseberry. i pick
a mountain lady slipper
and loop it in the lapel
of my daypack,
as we move through

boreal thickets,
bouldered splay
runnelled by
run-off, sapling
meadows, lake-
as-lick,

terrain varied,
slope gradual.

'am i
the only one
with wet feet?!'
Wayne wrings
out his socks from
his muck boots.
we are all in
the same boat.
quite literally.

and so begins
the sounds of
stih*l*ness ...

felling, limbing,
sweeping

we become
chain-gang of
clearing ...

re-tracing, missing,
re-routing and re-
routed by blazes

trees begin
to fall,
ranging in span
and radii of ring.
we enlarge breadth
and width *so a*
pannier-packer may pass through.
though in a park,
Wayne holds a
tenure which allows him
to maintain and
clean existing trail

or clear
an obstacle …

the lake
has risen an
estimated eight to ten feet.
the added volume
exceeding edges
in metred multiples of tens,

> *funnelling force*
> into river rush.
> *overtaking trees*

forcing detours.

this is all
legal.

our line
is careful
and considered …

> *even so, Wayne does quip :*
> 'this is not exactly
> leave-no-trace
> camping'

we end
up covering
nineteen kilometres
round-trip.
eight hours
out-and-back.
we clear just over half.

*i had my
walking poles,*
and took naproxen
before and at
lunch. *this is
the longest
distance i have
traipsed in the
last year.*

crooked steps.
hobbled legs.

> *'we were just
> talking about
> you ... you're
> really tough!'*

> *'i have a
> reputation
> for such!'*

> *'one tough
> babe!'*

> i accept
> the compliment
> with a smile

i will,
later,
prop my boots up,
upside down,

> *(treat my pickled-
> feet with anti-fungal
> cream)*

and

finally
sitting,

    wrap my
    fingers around
    the comfort
    of a cup of tea ...

6.

i am
humbled
ornithologically

    in my
    wanton desire

to discern
arc of avian
orchestra.

i demote
myself, in
dawn's chorus,
to mere
desirest of
avifaunal-attunement.
still, not yet,
even
novice ...

    i keep
    getting them
    wrong.

my audio-
graphic and phonic
aptitude lacking
in accuracy. *inaccuracy.*

i keep
listening.

but the birds have me beat.

a red squirrel
adds voice
to the tempoed
choir. i can make out
that chatter
without any doubt.
always.

pancakes and
bacon feature
on today's skillet-
grilled menu. there
is an excess of
bacon in camp :

       'does it still
       smell good?'

       'rinse it off.'

       'we'll use yours
       first.'

       '... and the cream?'

       'it's clotted, not
       curdled ...'

i will
not be
partaking.

instead,
i try to
placate a
growing swirl of anxiety
birthed from the realization

that i *may* have
poured my coffee into
my mug,
left out the night
before, without checking
it first.

i manage to
convince myself that
i did just that :

not check ...

> though the
> presence of
> rodents appears
> largely non-existent
> > *(yet, mice are*
> > *soon found amongst*
> > *the nearby saddles),*
>
> *even in the unlikely event*
>
> that i *did* ingest
> a dropping ...
> *pioneers, home-*
> *steaders, flop-housers,*
> *couch-surfers,* all
> would have
> inadvertently consumed a
> turd or two over the course
> of their lives, *surely*
> *with (little or) no consequence*
>
> especially cowboys.
>
> *but ...   once the anxiety is spiked,*
> *rational reasoning simply cannot reign*
> *back in the runaway thoughts ...*

a call-out breaks my growing, looping fear :

'i hear the horses.'

the wranglers
had been
canoed up-
lake, dropped
off, to now
return bareback
with the train …

> *the two adoptees*
> *never followed our*
> *herd when they*
> *hobbled off two nights ago.*
> the horse count
> is back to twenty-one.

after
all are haltered
and tied-to-
trees,

the *beautifully,*
and amply
tattooed farrier

and i,
sit and start
talking ink.
the focus turns to my
copper alchemy
imprint. she

mentions an ex
of hers had

wilson's disease,
too –
  a copper metabolizing
  disorder with neurological,
  hepatological, and psychiatric
  affects –
and suffered
from paranoia
as a result ...

  the confirmation
  that my struggles with a
  nervous mind – an *obsessive*
  compulsive disorder – currently
  manifesting as germaphobia –
  (usually irrational, yet rationally-
  prompted) are rooted
  in my neurological genetic
  disorder *both* serves to
  lessen
  the gut-churning
  grip, *while at the*
  same time,
  reinforces it.

  with little 'working
  memory' *(a byproduct*
  of the disease),
  i am unable to
  recall the moment
  of now-near-obsession.
  i cannot replay the cup-grabbing
  event in my head.
  i will, likely be able
  to access this information,
  to hit replay, in a
  day or two. but not
  now. not immediately.
  not when i need to.

when i need it most.
this gap is where
the worry creeps in,
widening the chasm

and

debilitating fear
takes hold ...

with trembling hands,
i braid my hair
and cuff cowpoke
snaps.

i still have
not been able
to help with
daily dish duties,
or meals, *despite*
my email claim
that i willingly
would do both ...

>   *(tomorrow i will be*
>   *called-out on such,*
>   *suggesting i*
>   *will be thought of*
>   *not as a team player)*

i explain.

>   *'you should*
>   *let people know.'*

i will.
i do (somewhat, a little, not enough,
barely).

i try. *in time.* i'm
not sure how.

> *i keep*
> *hand sanitizer*
> *on hand,*
> at all times.

i carry herbal tinctures.

[and i begin to withdraw.]

the 'new' trail
requires another
day of clearing …

files sharpen
blade of chainsaw
bar. gas gets
poured into
jerry can. oil
container double-
bagged.

i join,
> *despite the*
> *anxiety, despite*
> *the knee, despite*
> *the ability to be*
> *little more than*
> *a notetaking,*
> *flower-picking,*
> *endless-bird-call-*
> *asking, occasional-*
> *branch-moving help*

i pack
extra food. *i will
do my best to stuff the panic.*

.

the process
is deft, meticulous,
considerate

      *'it's just a twisted
      mess in here'*

      'mark that tree'

      *'i'm pretty sure that's
      the way we don't
      want to go'*

      *'i'll drop this one …
      i'm going to leave
      that one'*

      *'we made a new
      blaze to replace
      the one you just cut
      down'*

      'too big for my back'

      'we can't just roll it'

      *'give this one a push
      that way'*

'i sat in sap'

'saprophytes don't
photosynthesize'

'we're making
headway now'

'watch out!'

we landmark

      the politics, practice
      and protocols of *how,*
      when and/or *if*
      to sign the 'new' trail
      are discussed

lightness begins
to relieve the
lingering seize
of grey,

there exists
a liminal
quality to
the luminosity

      'can a poet-without-a-thesaurus
      ask a favour of you? could you
      please look up alternate words
      for clouds, for me?!'

[sent from : N 58.230819° W 124.336285° elevation : 890 m][23]

'billow scud pother nebula
murk mist puff veil gloom
steam vapour veil mare's tail.
brume pea soup sheep rack'

late afternoon,
the sun breaks through

hooves are re-shoed. *and*
re-shoed. a batch of
faulty nails have left
our farriers endlessly
frustrated. *shoes keep*
falling off, en masse.

tomorrow we will try to ride.
but again, without
the full string.

.

evening
engages a sharing
of stories

a circle,

as

sinking western rays
cast aglow a
re-established
tranquility to east
Tuchodi Lake …

and i find calm

7.

i am
cacophonous
alarm of
cloven-printed
crack,

      crash

right next
to tent

a bush push-
through ...

      cow
      and calf

moose,

      bough-breaking
      slip-into-swim ...

i bear witness to

an intimate
communication of
grunts and
strokes

      i think of
      my daughter.

      i grab my
      inreach.

it's 5:55 a.m.

.
.
.

i halter
and hackamore
my own horse :

    'steering and brakes'

i'm donning
camo and print
of plaid. *trucker*
hat. timberlands.
    quasi-cowgirl-kit.'
whistle around
my neck :

    'one short and one long'
    means dismount and walk.

    we do so,
    down a narrow,
    steep section.

leading Toni, we
manoeuvre downhill
    with a mutual understanding
of my restricted
movement capabilities.
we awkwardly, *and gently*
lean into the other ...

we work in

conjunction ...

    'good girl'

re-mounted,
her witherless
fifteen-five-or-
sixish-hands-highness
carries me
with a lightness
of ease.

the clandestine
cleave of heaven's
heave has relented.
it's bright,
warming.

clear.

        i strip down to bra,
        cupping a collection of
        needles
            (*raingear, however
            always compulsorily lashed
            to rear of saddle ...)

i reign
through
intagliated
leaf, verigation
of viscous tissue,
folliaged sgraffito

and the gossamer
of flight ...

fringed by wings.
everywhere.

i am tired.
the jingle
of salt-cube jostling
mixed with
stay-at-home
hobbling,
and sound of
first bird
     song *(unknown)*
at quarter-after-
three replaced
shut-eye with
light-of-night ...

now, saddle-
sitting,

     twisting turns
     with torso

i am
flanked by
butterwort
and larkspur.

     swivel round
     swing-back
     of switch,

as we
thorough
our trail re-awakening,
Wayne begins
to believe

this is more-
than-likely the
original way
into the lake :

> 'this is the one
> the First Nations
> would have used'

he recognizes
signs, sites.

> he refers to it
> more as a route,
> than a trail

even in our
re-'claiming',
it retains its
sense of
subtleness,
of belonging.

> and even though
> on thousand-
> pound beasts,

we still
tread lightly.

the path
does not
        (surprisingly)
feel scarred by

our *(anthropocentric)*-
axe and saw ...

> *more so,*
> > re-recognized

> as opposed to,
> > re-purposed,

> purposed anew.

> *arousing dormancy*

> aliven*ed*,

sap flows,
pitch patches.

we move
onto the
High Trail ...

> *'anyone have anything*
> *in their saddle bags*
> *they don't want to drown?'*

we stop before swale.

this is
our first
make-or-break
moment.
depth unknown.
we pass
through.

and so we do
the second
and third,
    stirrup-deep,
    boots mud-splattered :

'*we can*
get out of here now
and get up
the mountain'

today's farther-
reconnaissance-
ride has confirmed
we can pass
through the swales,
the up-until-now
potential
obstacle in our
hopeful
down-*instead-of*
cross-streaming
route.

    with the
thwart of our
initial expedition
plan, we will
now be able to travel
down river, then turn north,
instead of the initial plan *which was* :
ford water and head south ...

    we can
    return and
    prepare the packstring.

one week late,
turning in the opposite direction.

as we head back
to camp,
we roam through
stereo-scope of images,
cut-outs,
postcards :

    i become
    franked by
    this surface-
    mail

    my stamp :

one
of deepening
questions ...

    leverage of
    limestone,

    lifts the
    line of sight

i return,

    with saddlesore

and cradle
my sleep on

diatomaceous earth ...

8.

i am
blend
of brushed strokes

> *a palette of smudge*

vision hazing

this daily painting,

> shifting

distinction between

> expanse of above,
> precision of soaring precipice
> and bowl of freshwater ripple,

merging

.
.
.

incoming reports tell of
thousands of hectares ablaze :

> *'everything is on fire'*

> one hundred miles-
> *in a straight line*-away

the heat has returned.
and getting hotter ...

> *which could, again,*
> *mean water levels rising.*

today is a
camp day. *prepping panniers,*

> eyes keeping a close lookout on shifting shore and bank levels.

we prepare for one night riverside,
three above tree line.

.

.

.

lakeside,

i find
curlicue of shell,

a chronicler,

> *'time is a human construct.'*

> ... and we are fucking with it ...

> *'how long does it take to snow a mountain?'*

the day silhouettes
into a beautiful,

yet terrifying, wash.

smoke signals

     now that we can get up the mountain,
     will we see a view? what will we see?

river high, mountain low
burning the ocean floor

the kōan of bearing witness,
eyes open.

                    i set my alarm for 4:30 ...

9.

i am
[a] quick-release
knot of a
pre-dawn routine :

    neck handkerchiefed
    and ponytailed

over, through, back, across,
square off your diamond,
tighten the slack, notch,
cinch, hoist, lasso, lash ...
pull.

    aviators on

raven calls

Toni is embossed in leather,
silver tasseled florettes,
embellished with copper stud.
blazed and black maned, i
groom her stripe of back, two
left white socks and three
right freckles.

    'your saddle's
    a heavy one!'

the sky pinks.

horses dapple
the trees like bark

pairs of panniers
are weighed to be
within a pound of
each other. horse-
backs are affixed
with wooden
sawbucks and the
load is prepared, along
with rope-wrapped
canvas soft packs :

    'what did you put on Hank?'

    'the table.'

    'and not the kitchen?!'

Lockit has rubbed himself
loose of his halter. Comet
has been savagely bug-
bitten *(the automatic*
transmission fluid-as-insect
repellent being applied –
dabbed behind the ears –
and rationed until next
re-supply). Bob and Don
are drafted for size. and
Rosie will be ridden.

we pack, stash and cache.
coolers, hockey bags and
ammo kit *(full of steel*
shoes) are hauled up high

into spruce. i tie and belay
the bulky loads from the
bottom. after all is secured,
a bag begins to leak ... *alcohol* ...
the ultimate attractant ...

'where's the binder twine?'

the morning's
camp dismantle and
loading assembly takes
roughly four-and-
a-half hours.

> *we review*
> *whistle signals :*

> > *1 – stop*
> > *2 – go*
> > *3 – stop and come help*

Gataga carries my gear.

'LET'S RIDE!'

> lead saddle
> is slung with axe,
> rear with gun.

we pass
again through
our old new trail,

through tussock,
over hillock. columbine
and yet-to-bloom ambit
of fireweed.

> Mongo, Ronnie and
> Jack *renegade the line,*
> being the only three
> without pack or rider.
> *they budge, nudge,*
> *gallop ...* they adventure

we get off
trail. we regain
trail. deviate,
re-direct.

my bareback,
lined with spray
of swale-fording
mud. my arms,
branded by branch.
crotch, *chafed raw* :

> [*thongs *are not* appropriate
> for *this* kind of leg splay.]

three blows of the
whistle from the
front find two
wranglers, from
the rear, dismounting
and running full speed
ahead. Buddy's panniers
have slipped under his
belly.

we will stop
here for lunch.

we eat, riverside.
    three-and-a-half
    hours after leaving.
this is where we
rode to, two days
previous. as we are
making good time,
we are steered
towards the alpine ...

    'now we have to
    find the trail ...'

the mertensia
of bluebells
directs us up

hind haunches
begin beading,
then streaming
sweat.

cotton seeds the stick of humidity.

    'high of 26 today, 27 tomorrow'

    'thunderstorm?'

    'doesn't say'

    'that's definitely a thundercloud.
    you can have all your sciencey

stuff you want ... but i know how
to read the sky ...'

soundbites crisp the air,

while *this* landscape
    beyonds my dictionary,

and personal
threshold of thesaurus :

    'words for sky please'
        [sent from : N 58.300554° W 124.285751° elevation : 1,539 m]

    'atmosphere   stratosphere   the skies   airspace   heavens
    firmament   vault of heaven   the blue   wide blue yonder
    the welkin   the ether   the empyrean   the azure
    the upper regions   the sphere'

we gain elevation.

i spur
a coaxing
'c'mon girl'
with my heel

grasses lea us
through filter
of forest flower.
sieve
of softness.

'looks like we came up
the wrong trail.

we're supposed
to be over there
            [Wayne points]

but i know how
to get us there ...
                maybe not today.'

from atop,
we look down
into layers of
valley, foreground,
background, *all*
around :

        Toni's saddle,
        ironically, is made
        in High River

we have
just come up
the 'wrong' mountain ...

        this, our kōan.

.
.
.

due to the incline,
we must walk
the horses down.
i will walk on my

own, without
leading Toni.
with today's grade,
today's heat, the same
rule doesn't apply
as last time : *'you can
stay on. you barely
weigh anything, i doubt
she really even notices
you're there.'* i am
farrier-fashioned a
walking stick. i remove
bridle, tie rope to horn.

Toni will not deviate. she
will stay in line. i
go to the end of
the train and haul
ass as a caboose,
*for three kilometres
straight downhill* losing
the roughly 300 metres
we just gained.
two stay back with
me. once down,
Wayne asks how
that was :

> *'well, there are cowpoke,
> and then there's the slowpoke'*

> *'you're not slow. not at all.
> you might think you're slow
> compared to what you used
> to be … but you're not!'*

i re-pitch
my tent beside

ionic flow
of hydraulics :

    positive generators.

daisies
deliver my doorstep.

and from
my front door ...

        an elk.

10.

i am
alpined

    implicated by
    my inextricability

riding
the same line
as this land,

    precariously fragile,
    resilient as fuck

deeply entrenched
in a continuum of
knowing ...

    this is
    sedimentary

elementary

    here,
    especially,

    time implodes

context takes over concept

i am
property of
proximal distancing
    [see *day 13*]
(un)distancing proximity

i become
who *i am* :

        a range of views

.
.
.

'let's go, let's go!'

i mount
at eight. awake
since 3:30. had
my site struck
and was coffeed
well-before five.

i'm sporting dirty,
broken fingernails
in fingerless gloves,
        creasing soft with use.
i'm back to braids.

a moving sweep
of cloud cover comes,
clings, then clears

Lockit loads my
'featherlight' boxes.
Levi wears the champion
bull rider saddle. the axe
is slung on Titus. Mongo
has his own private rodeo.
Toni objects the whole
way up to he-who-is
behind-her. *she keeps
taking several steps
back.* she holds no qualms,
however, about using the
rump in front as a scratching
post. *double standard.*
and Tuchodi remains
his steady self, constantly
composed.

*monkshood and
paintbrush appear
with incline.*

i sip sky and
swallow sip.

*whisky jack
heralds our
gain in height.*

  i look back,
  looking forward

we find
a piece of flat,
        amongst roll of folds,
sited above
creek,

krummholz level,

cratered by *saddles-
of-scree,*

> where porousness
> seeps through
> lineation of
> sheep trail

i pick
up conglomeration
of quartz,

> i look forward,
> looking back

.
.
.

*'the country
won't hold the horses'*

> up here, there
> is not enough forageable
> food to sustain
> the herd. *we had hoped
> there would be.*

a decision is made.
we will
be dropped off and
the horses driven
back down riverside,
by the wranglers :

'we're taking a pot and
a saucepan ... and a lid!'

we are
to be retrieved and reunited
with the packtrain
after two nights ...

    'and that was the
    last we saw of them!'

    'i think we'll call this
    after the battle'

    'half hour of chaos
    for two hours of peace'

    'not much plot,
    but lots of action.'

we are
summer saxifraged,
campioned by
moss and rung by
jacob's ladder.

a horsefly
draws blood.
then another.

breeze turns to
wind, necessitating
stake-down of shelter
nestled in purple, pink, yellow ...

i wander
up a rising
sweep of hill
with another,

      our lungs tugging
      in the lift

      of altitude

i kneel
my face in stream.

i will later bed under
loft of mare's tails,

            dreaming entomological ~~dreams~~ nightmares ...

11.

i am
bloodbathed
within
murderous
streak,

fly-trapped
o-positive meshed

> *'these are the worst*
> *bugs we've seen in years*
> *and years and years'*

i transfuse

my nighted niche
set amongst border
of blooms was
at the expense of
slant and stone-
to-spoon ...

> *my body welcoming*
> *the curl of curvature*

i spot
a spruce-topped
golden-crowned
sparrow

bearberry carpets
in verdancy that which
will soon fall crimson.
blue-turning-berry stipples, while

dwarf nagoons flower
the display

in collapsible
chair, next to
table clothed in
coffeemate and
china lily, leftover
chili and cornbread,
i ready boots and
bottles. *and a*
long sleeve shirt.

today, we hike.
again.

we uphill
through rock
which *'predates*
shelly creatures' ...

i opt
not to scramble
up cirque-of-scree
to bits of wrecked
fuselage,

>   *i wince at its*
>   *glint from creek-*
>   *side florescence*

i glory
in the expanse
of limitless

aloneness ...

.

.

.

i shit
for the first time
in four days. i
cover my deposit
with *crystalline*
vug. it seems
appropriate in a
place which holds

> *composites of present*
> *passings in tandem*
> *with the accumulation*
> *of many yesterday's ...*

the largest of the
local ungulates has
recently
moved through.
i smile with the
thought that this
trip has earned me
a somehow-absurdly-
apt-*yet-out-of-*
context signifier – one of
a particular flavour of
ice cream : *moose*
tracks.
       i consider
who i might want to
share it with ...

the man i'm
desperately trying
to fall myself
out of love with,
or the man, i am
having to admit,
i find myself thinking about
more and more frequently,
or ...

i wonder
about my heart's
capacity to hold

i wear it strapped to
my sleeve,

      but here i sit,

                shirtless,
                sleeveless

                      (*in a bug-relieved breeze)

i consider
how your heart
is the size of
your fist,

      my hands,

             petite

      with deep
      lifelines :

which manage
to beat with the
pulse of the

earth,

and so too,
carry the weight
of the world …

heartleaf
arnica pushes up,

and
a butterfly
lands upon me

i lay
back,

cushioned

i am held,

here.

'alone'

behind me,
tumble of landslide.
erosion of eons,
crumble of
centuries …

nearing.

passages and
partings, makings
and takings parsed
in hum, thrum,
vapour and
vanishing points …

i am
enmeshed in
animacy

> *enacted, felt,*
> *realized*

againing my
always,

anew,
> *in situ …*

smoke haze
dulls distance
with aura of
eerie prophecy.
foretelling a fiery
future,

> purgatory of
> progress …

i am
the land
of echoes

orientation
plies, burying
sightlines in
wrap of ridge,
collapsing into
disappearance,
retreat and upon-
ing ... *always beckoning*

     a closer farther,
     nearer far ...

.

.

.

i am
later
rejoined

together,
     we saturate
     within sensuousness

the side-of-
mountain-crash
left only metal and
a manual

on how to run a
high-caliber
machine gun

i cup
river from
stream,

      and as bumblebees
      pollinate
      this perennialness

i spot
      forget-me-nots ...

12.

i am
new mooned
by beading ball
of rising red

> my head fills with bruce cockburn
> lyrics. indeed the world
> has survived into another day.

> ablaze

> he and i both finding reason
> to think about eternity.[24]

mixed breeds

of

appaloosa, quarter horse,
percheron, belgian and
palomino, painted, bayed
and greyed

appear over rise

>   ... 'they're coming!'

blackened pots, caffeine
press, oil cloth and wash
basins are properly stacked
and stowed,

talc is sought to
treat stick of leather.
harness of britchen,
attached and fastened.

we are
about to begin
a slow, steady
stampeding down
of a barely discernable
single-track, *narrowing
through narrow.*

*Wayne whoops us
to the ready*

Kylo packs the oil and
gas. Hank tries to throw
his weight around : '*don't
be a bully.*' and yet-to-be-
string-broken Mongo
becomes a bucking bronco,
careening off at a gallop,
disappearing over edge :

> '*i do prefer shaken
> not stirred.*'

he just
happens to be carrying
my panniers ...

> i am
> beginning
> to learn the names
> of the string

and their personalities …

Mongo is coaxed
back in line. he
enters behind Toni,
much to her insistent
displeasure. she gives
him every opportunity
to pass, which he refuses.
he tows the Toni line.

> *'you can keep riding
> as long as your saddle
> doesn't slip forward.'*

> i sit back.
> it doesn't.

> *posture perfecting
> my shadow.*

my secondhand
shady brady
straw cowboy hat
brims my eyes,
resting over
still-unwashed
hair — *'it looks so
good'* — and my
iridescent festival
fanny pack, packing
pepperoni, power bars
and painkillers.

we authentize
the steeplechase :

    rugged
    rough
    real

the dressage
of down :

    dirt, dust, muck,
    water crossings,
    hurdle of fallen
    log, beds of boulder,
    pushback of brush,
    uproot of windthrow

i blow
a single whistle

stop,

sending it up
the line in succession.
Jack has
gone awol :

    'he's not on the
    spectrum …

    he's on a
    different spectrum'

we are
en route back to
Tuchodi Lake,
back to camp.

when we first arrived,
days ago,
to our alpine perch,
i noticed a particular
slice of stone,
perpendicularly
set,
protruding an inch or so
from the trail. it felt
different,

placed,
intentional.

early this morning,
before commencing our
five+ hours on horseback,
we gathered under

cirro-sky :
a pillow of prefixes :

talking,
observing.

Wayne pointed
to the rock. he,
too, remarked on
its features,
how it could potentially
be a hearth stone.
both he and i,
felt and recognized
the same thing …

today, we will
again, pass back
through 'our' new-
old trail. i think ahead,
of how in this one
particular place,
every time in passing,
i sense bones. *beneath*
mound. reminding me of
presence past, whispering
this wild alive ...

.

.

.

we lower
through *biologically layered*
strata,

    whites of yarrow
    and bistort flag our departure

though
not plentifully obvious,
mushrooms and mycelia appear.
morchella, esculenta, trametes. whilst,
visibly elusive, their networking
sustains this emergence :

    location-specific

coolness pulls
up the cover.
i begin to yawn at the
tail end of
the ride ...
>   the expression
>   of an accumulation
>   of day-lit nights.
>   one after the other.
>   i am
>   running on (near)
>   empty.

we arrive
back to the lake
and camp,
late afternoon.

the picturesque
has been absconded by
bass-blaring, gun-
shooting, drive-by-
boating. *the peace
broken into redneck
pieces.* at least our
site remains
unoccupied.

i am
extremely
stiff, and dismount
in such a way
that my necklace
gets hung up on
the horn. *it
doesn't break.*
i am strung up,
feet dangling,
full weight on

chain. Wayne
happens by,
lifting me out of predicament.

'there's no doubt
you're tough'
           a wrangler will utter

however,
this i have been
feeling less and less
as this trip's progressed ...

after yesterday's
solo meadow-
morning,

i felt replenished,
recalibrated and inspired to go back

'and do every dish in camp ...'

and yet, (almost predictably) the
pendulum of sensitivity swung
and i fell victim to the debilitation
of a panic attack. no dishes
were soaked or soaped. *my*
'toughness' resting, and revealed,
solely in my vulnerability. i talk.
i type : satellite text. i reach out :

           'you are one
           of the strongest
           women i know
           and everything
           you have experienced
           before this has

prepared you for
what's ahead.
you already know
that though.
stay tough'

the anxiety
begins to disperse ...

.

.

.

the lake
begins to pound,
breaking.
there is now a slight shore.
sand. feet of beach.
and yet, it is still high.
very. dinnertime
conversation revolves
around comparison
and conversion of
volumes :

> *'how many acre-feet*
> *are in a hectare-metre?'*

i, again, pitch
my tent. clinging
fiercely to it,
erected, airborne.
i use every peg,
extend both

vestibules, as it
windsocks.

we do not erect
the tarp.

today is new moon.
it occurs precisely
at 6:19 p.m. at this
time, i am beholden
    to a
long-distance
photography-
cum-performance
project i am
undertaking in
collaboration with another[25] ...

for it,
i don white slip
and streak of
white paint.
i blaze it down
my face like

my equine
    friend, my support

upon whom,
a sense of
contemplative
equanimity
is easily cultivated,

i find her,
hobbling off,

and,
with our shared physical
imbalance of legs

i snap our
picture. together.

on each new moon,
the project asks me
to answer anew :

'*what am i birthing?*'

in this shared moment,
i find my answer :

art.

and

honesty.

connection.

indivisible from
(my) life

that which
captures and
strives to find
means to express,
to distill,
to understand

enlarging,
entrophying,
encapsulating
and
embodying

the complexities,
and transparency
of *my*

    'i am'

        here, in place.
          together.

13.

i am
launder
of lap,
quick-dipped
in the chop —

> *change of*
> *wind direction*

lave of south-
west to -east

> *cleansed*
> *by chill*

i stand naked
within air's breath

> *expunge*
> *of lung*

looking, *as i dress*,
directly at the sun,
unveiling momentarily
through shroud

> *luminescent*
> *pearl*

dragonflies swirling,
butterweed burgeoning

i wildcraft
fruit of strawberry ...

       am served
       meal of moose

.
.
.

i walk
alone,
and visit an
old Indigenous
camp,

i reflect
on my relationship
to notions of peripheries

       of being,
       or feeling, peripheral ...

i have felt
so embraced
by this land,

not separate
from it :

       accepted. welcome.

       fostered by my sheer
       curiosity, my questioning,
       my wondering, want ...

my desire for, and
commitment to,
understandings,

my noticing.

intrinsically, innately,
intuitively kneaded
by this place,

imploding peripheries
of an 'unknown' …

all, but my own.

i have been
a contradiction
to my own hope
and intention.

i have, sadly,
ironically, been
completely
        peripheral
to the very process

permitting me access
to this place.

i have been disconnected –
in a more traditional sense
of the word – from the going-
ons of camp –
        the hub, the cog –
from which all of this

'horsing around'
extends

i have been
on the periphery
of packstring prep,
chores, shakedown and
takedown ...

before coming,
i knew this might,
inevitably,
become a possibility ...

but i had not anticipated to such an extent.

i, clearly,
struggle with
anxiety.
i had gotten *just*
ahead of it,
managing it to the
point of near-eradication,
where it was no longer
significantly impacting
or inhibiting my behaviour, my habits.
this, *however,*
is put to the test and can be exacerbated
in group or social situations,
when exhausted or
after extreme sun exposure :

the only newbie rider in the group,
i have not been sleeping, i am physically-
limited, and my skin has been reddened
and darkened considerably.

i am failing the test.

before coming,
i had also made the decision
not to participate in camp meals.
i wanted to maintain my consumption
of an ethically-sourced, predominantly-
organic, non-processed, unrefined,
sugar-free diet. and one that didn't
produce a lot of waste. *though i would*
miss out on the communality of sharing
food, after watching the amounts of
packaged, instant carbs and perishable
foods eaten a wee-bit-too-long post-
refrigeration, i am pleased i stuck
to this resolve. to make up for this
decision, *in the same group email*
in which i explained i would not be
participating in shared meals, i did
declare that i would willingly help
with food prep and kitchen duties.
i genuinely hoped, and planned to
do so, having written such from a
strong, settled 'place', where that
felt totally possible. normal.

i had set this as an intention :

> *pushing my peripheries,*
> limited in the past two
> years by the emergence
> of my disease-induced
> phobic tendencies.

i didn't want to set myself apart,
before even leaving —

but,
because i had announced this
compensatory 'offer,'

the fact was that i soon
would become incapable
of upholding it, became
uncomfortable,
          distressing,
                    (self)isolating

                    at first, i felt it best to
                    observe, as opposed to
                    interfere with the well-
                    oiled equine machine. i deemed
                    this the best way to later
                    integrate seamlessly.
                    i deemed wrong.

                    i lost my chance.
                    my back-benching backfired.
                    i had shot myself in the foot.
                    my retreat serving to work
                    myself out of the open window,
                    i had inadvertently framed,

                              and latched.

my scope of helping
with the horses was
limited as well –
again, i did not know
the intricacies of routine –
with my movement
impaired, i was limited
with what i could learn,
sling or swing. *i did try*
to participate here more
readily :

distributing feed muzzles,
folding and stacking blankets,
holding a horse

small tasks.
little jobs.

but this was
not for want, or
lack of,
engagement,

     connection,

with Toni :

     strong-willed and quirky,
     kind, gentle, sensitive Toni …

Wayne says
he aims to match
horse with rider.

in this case,
he chose the perfect fit.

.
.
.

     'she likes you!'

.
.
.

i began
to wonder
just *how, when,*
if to communicate
what was going on for me
with the others
      [this, i never quite
      resolved].
i wasn't deliberately
trying to set myself apart, quite the contrary.

the fact that i *was,*

entrenched a sense of
guilt, awkwardness.
i had to confront
my estrangement :

      i began to empower
      my peripheral
      observations by
      focusing on my writing –

            rarely seen without
            pen and paper

      i privately rationalized,
      and justified, my
      different form of (in)active
      involvement
                with the hope
      that my words
      would be some form of
      after-the-fact, delayed
      offering to the group ...

      timescales,
      after all,

here,

avail themselves to more
open interpretations.

i graced
myself with
this permission.
i had to. it was
my *only* saving
grace.

i emphasized
connection in
other ways,

to become

that 'property of
proximal distancing
[*see day 10*]
(un)distancing proximity' :

to unperipherize
my shrinking peripheries

i engaged conversations,
i continuously asked questions ...

all the while
asking questions of myself ...

.

.

.

after standing
naked,

    exposed

[lakeside]

    i return

[to camp]

and willingly join in
the feasting
of freshly-made
Bannock

breaking bread together,

        i feed my soul …

14.

i am
braless
and base
layered

as i

jetboil the chill
into covet of
coffee steam :

> *'this most popular
> girl in camp'*

the fuel cannister frosts

wranglers return
with the horses :

> seven have been
> unhobbled sometime
> during the night.
> there is total disbelief
> and upset in the air.

> we decide to pay the riverboat
> camp a visit,

when we travel through,
westward :

> today's soon-to-
> be-and-final-ride.

i sit Toni for what
will be the
last time.

     i have
     finally
     been broken
       [finally broken]

     legs molding
     around roan,
     sitz bones becoming
     cushion for concave of
     leather, legs stirruped with
     an ease of
     positioning

we feel good together

     'i'm going to miss her'

  .
  .
  .

we draw into next-of-trail
sprawl of jetboat-camp tents.

Wayne rides forward with a
'good morning.' he
slings one leg over
front, adopting a casual,
conversational position …

all the while, i notice,
he has [completely
unintentionally]
revealed the rifle
side-saddle-strapped,
barrel exposed through
scabbard. he says
we are looking for
some lost hobbles.
the guys do mention
the horses woke them up.
they offer little more. *we do
not accuse.* we
merely draw the parallel that
this is as upsetting to
us, as if someone were to, say,

come untie a jetboat in
the middle of the
night ...

*they don't give us their names,
though Wayne cordially offers
his.*

we half expect/
hope to find the
hobbles left out,
on our way back
through.

we don't.

.

.

.

swallowtails and
brushfoots filter
light above blanket
of bryophyte,

through burl
of bark and buffaloberry

a chickadee chirps.

the lake is lowering.

hugging shore,
we ribbon our way

weaving amongst
whorl of wood onto
isthmus of point.
we soak in

> *'visuals to hang onto*
> *for a lifetime'* ...

incisor gnash
of sharp,

cavity capture
of pocketed
sun-glazed ice,

> *wisdom*

from the mouth
of mountains ...

.
.
.

a black wing-
tipped gull

the white-
and-blackness
of loon [again,
               alone]

*... and then i spot
a feather*

someone whips
off their horse and
gathers it for me ...

i softly sing
myself home ...

we don't know
what we've got
'til it's gone ....

15.

i am
bindle bag of

moveable home,

a sense of place

sense of home

moveable place

palms in waking lake,

raven flies
a circle
around me

i am
ovulating

impregnated
here

i hold
found fossil,
touch its
corraline
segments,

an umbilical
connection :

genetically
geological

related.

.

.

.

i spend
time with Toni

      eyes locked,

we have become
each other's whisperer

      'thank you for taking me past my breaking point.'

i step
away
not wanting
to leave

i remove my cowboy shirt
i retain the hat …
      i will be returning *back* to this *country*

before i board,

a photograph

is taken of my
legs

    'no one said you weren't tough ...

    see you on the trail!'

still crooked,

my heart remains in, and with, the Muskwa-Kechika ...

epilogue

expedition | ɛkspɪ'dɪʃ(ə)n |

noun
1 a journey undertaken by a group of people with a particular purpose, especially that of exploration, research, or …

.
.
.

2 a write-of-passage …

.
.
.

∪

endnotes

1 Akrigg, G.P.V. and Helen (1988), *British Columbia Place Names* Sono Nis Press: Victoria, BC. Pg. 97.

2 Excerpt from the Fort Nelson First Nation Membership Code: http://www.fortnelsonfirstnation.org/information.html

3 Both the official MKMA website and the Akrigg's book indicate that Muskwa means 'black bear' in Cree. However, I also came upon this information in the book *Northern British Columbia Canoe Trips* (Rocky Mountain Books, 2010) by Laurel Archer: 'Though indeed Muskwa means "black bear" in that language [Cree], it is more likely the name of the river is derived from the Slavey name Mah Qua and that that was the name of the hunter with territorial rights to the river. On an 1895 map of the Muskwa River was labelled "Sicannie River," but in 1914 the Geographic Board of Canada adopted "Muskwa River." A 1917 BC land map called it the Musqua River. The notes on the BC Geographical Names Information System (BCGNIS) website state: "The only name which the Indians recognize is the Musquah. The custom apparently is for a separate band of the Sikanni Indians to hunt on [one and only one] of these and the rivers receive the names of the leaders in each band – thus Musquah's River, Prophet's River, Sikanni Chief's River and Fantasque's River." This information was taken from the report of Major E.B. Hart, who participated in 1912 Department of Lands survey of the Liard River. According to George Behn, a past chief of Fort Nelson First Nation, the name Muskwa is derived from the Slavey name Mah qua.' (pg. 320)

4 Referencing 'Burden' by Foy Vance.

5 Authored by Wayne Sawchuk, Northern Images, 2004.

6 Authored by G.P.V. and Helen Akrigg (see endnote i)

7 Authored by Sydney and Richard Cannings and JoAnne Nelson, Greystone Books, 2011.

8 Authored by Donna Kane, Harbour Publishing, 2018.

9 Was listening to 'Out There' podcast, episode 'The Ultimate Outdoorswoman', June 16, 2021.

10 Akrigg, G.P.V and Helen (see endnote i), pg. 311.

11 These excerpts were taken from various pages on the following site: https://www.muskwa-kechika.com.

12 Pannier is pronounced 'pan-yr' – as 'no self-respecting cowboy would ever pronounce them [phonetically spelled *panje*]'.

13 A hobble is a specifically designed piece of rope looped between the two front legs of a horse, to slow them down, to prevent straying, essentially 'hobbling' them.

14 'The Henry Foundation for Botanical Research offers 50 acres of beautiful gardens, plants, and wonderful views. Founded in 1948 by botanist and plant explorer Mary Gibson Henry (1884-1967) to showcase the plants she collected on her expeditions through remote areas of the West, Midwest and Southeast, the Henry Foundation encompasses 50 acres of a surprisingly remote site in the steep hills of Gladwyne [Pennsylvania, USA] near the Schuylkill River.' https://tools.bgci.org/garden.php?id=2510?id=2510.

15 Of note, following my 2018 hike of the Nootka Island Trail, I visited the New York Museum of Natural History the following year. The museum houses (in its basement vaults) the Yuquot whaling shrine that was removed from its original location on Nootka Island by anthropologists. I relate my desire to visit the Henry Foundation, to this same experience. It somehow makes it come full circle.

16 http://go2mk.ca.

17 "Mary Henry: Pioneer Botanist of the Northern Rockies" by V.C. Brink and R.S. Silver (1996) in British Columbia Historical News produced by British Columbia Historical Federation. Pgs. 16-17. https://open.library.ubc.ca/collections/bch/items/1.0190635#p19z-5r0f.

18 I first heard this expression used by writer Robert McFarlane.

19 "Tectonostratigraphic Framework of the Mesoproterozoic Muskwa Assemblage, Northern British Columbia" by D.G.F. Long and J.R. Devaney, Department of Earth Sciences, Laurentian University. The latter part of this citation references (Pratt, 1998; Furniss et al., 1998). https://www.researchgate.net/profile/Darrel-Long-2/publication/286706581_Tectonostratigraphic_framework_of_the_Mesoproterozoic_Muskwa_assemblage_northern_British_Columbia/links/57446c6108ae9ace-841fe03e/Tectonostratigraphic-framework-of-the-Mesoproterozoic-Muskwa-assemblage-northern-British-Columbia.pdf.

20 https://bcparks.ca/explore/parkpgs/n_rocky/.

21 http://treaty8.bc.ca/treaty-8-accord/.

22 http://treaty8.bc.ca/home/2006-treaty-8-accord-declaration-of-bc-treaty-8-first-nations/.

23 Satellite messages sent using a Garmin inReach.

24 Referencing 'Wondering Where the Lions Are' by Bruce Cockburn.

25 An article with a selection of images about the collaborative project titled 'Birthing A/New' can be found at: https://tidsskrift.dk/peripeti/article/view/135198. At the time of printing, dates were being finalized for gallery exhibitions-cum-performance space events.

about the author

bronwyn preece is honoured to have the privilege of living on the unceded Traditional Territories of the Lílwat7úl and Skwxwú7mesh Peoples in whistler, british columbia. this awareness brings with it many levels of responsibility, humbleness,

transparency and collaborative possibilities. she is a multi-disciplinary, community-engaged arts practitioner. she holds a PhD in performance, along with an MA and BFA in applied theatre. she has taught, facilitated workshops, and performed internationally. her publications range from academic chapters to children's books. she is the author of *Gulf Islands Alphabet* (2012) and *Sea to Sky Alphabet* (2023). all of her artistic and educational work aim towards cultivating place-based awarenesses and small acts of reconciliatory repair. bronwyn is an avid, solo, backcountry backpacker who writes on the trail. she has the word *gratitude* tattooed on her arm …